PROPERLY PERCEIVED

Kimberly ♡

Zephaniah 3:17

Kimberly Underwood

ISBN 978-1-64559-814-5 (Paperback)
ISBN 978-1-64559-815-2 (Hardcover)
ISBN 978-1-64559-816-9 (Digital)

Covenant Books, Inc.
11661 Hwy 707
Murrells Inlet, SC 29576
www.covenantbooks.com

This humble book is dedicated to my Lord and Savior, Jesus the Christ. Whose love for me is unmeasurable, who took my place on the cross as atonement for my sins so that I might live an abundant life, not just in Heaven but here on earth! A life abundantly full of love, joy, peace, forgiveness and kindness. I'm eternally grateful, may this meager effort bring Him extraordinary Praise and Glory!

Properly Perceived

How do you perceive the world around you? Have you ever stopped to think that your perspective on things makes a significant difference? Do you realize the origin of your perspective, how it was shaped and the power of its impact on your life? God's Word gives us all the perspective we need for our lives here on earth and for eternity. Being able to better understand His perspective, the Kingdom perspective, you will begin to look at your life, the things of this world and the people around you in a very different way, you will begin to see things through God's glasses.

I challenge you to search God's Word and ask God for His outlook on things, seeking for God's Will to be done in your life over your own. In addition, you will begin to see the struggles, pain, and suffering in this world as only temporary and your opportunity to be sharpened and strengthened for the Kingdom of God. Ultimately, you will begin to see yourself and others through God's glasses, keeping in mind that you will never lay eyes on a human being that God does not love and that Jesus did not die for. This will completely change the way you treat people. You'll come away with a new understanding and a world more properly perceived.

GOD'S WILL
NOT YOUR OWN

Romans 12:2 (NIV) tells us that we are not to conform to the patterns (beliefs, understandings, points of view) of this world, but we are to be transformed by the renewing of our mind (changing our mindset by changing our perspective). Then, we will be able to test and recognize what God's Will is—His good, pleasing, and perfect Will. In order to be able to do God's Will we must first understand Him better, but more importantly, trust Him more. You cannot understand anyone unless you spend a great deal of time with them, listening to what they have to say, studying them, empathizing with them, and putting yourself in their shoes. We do this with God by spending time with Him, reading His Word, and seeking to understand His perspectives, what He's done for us and why He's done it and looking closely at His heart. In order to do that, you have to believe every word of the Bible to be true or what is the point? Start with faith, a full belief in things you cannot touch or see.

We also need to spend time with Him in our everyday lives. We talk with Him, sharing our thoughts, needs, concerns, fears, as well as, our hopes and dreams. In a close relationship with Him, we begin to build trust and a desire to be in His Will. Shortly, we will begin to rely on Him instead of our own understanding and inclinations. We begin to understand that He wants to be involved in ALL aspects of our lives and every single decision, even the teeny tiny ones. He proves Himself all together worthy to be involved in every minute of every day. Walking with Him in this way builds our confidence, enthusiasm, and faith. The worries and the cares of this world begin to fade away as we see how faithful He is. The emphasis we had on the worldly things around us start to fade and what is true, meaningful, and pleasing to God is what takes their place. We soon realize that nothing else matters and the things of this world become properly perceived.

LIFE GOES BY IN THE BLINK OF AN EYE

Have you ever stopped to think about why humans, no matter how well they take care of themselves, still age and pass on? Well, the truth is that God tells us in His Word that His intention was to walk with us on earth forever until we blew it, starting with Adam and Eve. That's when the fall of man began and we could no longer experience the relationship with God we once had or the eternal human body. Our lives became riddled with pain, suffering and hard work. This was our choice, not His. The rest of God's Word shows us how He continually pursues a relationship with us and how mankind can never make amends for his sin. God sent so many messengers throughout scriptures pleading with mankind to change his ways and follow God. The bottom line is...we wouldn't do it! So God lovingly sent His Son Jesus to make amends for us, to take our place in the seat of judgment and to pay the price for our sin. With His great gift we can now, once again, walk with God in a close relationship and, although we still face the frailties of this world, He has sent us His Holy Spirit as a guide and comforter.

Our human bodies will give out on us one day and we will pass on to the next life, so which one should you be more focused on? Your short time on earth or the life you can expect for eternity? If we are going to focus on eternity then we must have a Kingdom perspective in our lives now. We must see everything in the light of how it affects the Kingdom of God. Not consumed by what is happening here on earth but how the way we live our lives now is affecting our eternal lives and the eternal lives of those around us. How liberating it is to know that God wants to be in control of what happens to you on earth. Desiring His Will over your own allows a peace and certainty that you are striving for what really matters, eternity with Him, not just for yourself but for all those you touch along the way. The only thing you can take with you is other people! So can you see how nothing else here matters? It's all meaningless in the light of eternity. Here begins the journey of a making sure the things of this world are properly perceived.

THE REASON IS PAIN

Pain and suffering are a part of being separated from God in this fallen world here on earth. We all experience it and we all are trying to deal with the reality of it. Most of us cope with pain and suffering in destructive ways which we are not even aware of. Have you ever stopped to think that most of your wrong choices have come about as you were trying to ease your own pain and suffering? These poor choices are self-destructive, pain produces more pain, the more you are hurting the more desperate you grow trying to relieve it; therefore, you create more pain in your life.

This world has many 'remedies' for pain, things that promise self-worth, self-esteem, happiness, and peace, such as, physical beauty, wealth, power, fame/popularity, physical pleasures, and even things that seem like they are good for us, like focusing on yourself, centering yourself, or escaping from stress by trying to find a place of tranquility. However, these things do not fulfill you and the pleasures are only temporary. Once again, if we are focused on Him, His Will and His Kingdom, we are able to have a different view on the difficulties of this world. We will begin to understand that if we have invited Him into our lives, asked forgiveness of our sins, and chosen to follow the example that Jesus set for us, we can be sure to know that any suffering that comes while we are on earth is only temporary and God can use it for our good and the good of the Kingdom. It gives us the chance to glorify Him to all those around us as they watch how we cope with difficulty. We start to make better choices, ones that do not come from a desperate pursuit to relieve our pain but a desire to be holy before God and to reveal His Glory to others. The big picture, God's Kingdom, will help us properly perceive the challenges of this world and keep them from destroying who God intends us to be for His Kingdom. We will see the pain and suffering through new lenses.

SEEING OTHERS THROUGH GOD'S GLASSES

Once you have focused on God's Will for your life and His eternal Kingdom, you will have a completely different perspective on those around you. You will better understand their suffering, hopelessness, greed, anger, and self-centeredness, when you better understand that is who we all are without God. What you are seeing in other people is simply their state of being; they are in rebellion against God and are suffering without His presence in their lives. You will have far more compassion and patience for others, as you begin to see them as God sees them, as His lost sheep that He loves and desires to be with. You will be better able to show God's love to them and have a greater capacity to forgive. In addition, you will also be better equipped to hold others accountable, speak the truth in love and not enable or contribute to their wrong doings and poor choices.

As you walk closer with God, obeying Him and desiring His ways, you will begin to also desire the Fruits of the Spirit and they will be given in abundance to all those who ask Him. These character traits, as described in Galatians 5:22–23 (NIV): love, joy, peace, forbearance, kindness, goodness, faithfulness, gentleness, and self-control can only be found in God. No matter how hard we try, we humans cannot muster up the strength to fully and completely represent these traits in our lives but they become second nature the more we desire to be like Jesus and focus on God's Kingdom. These traits are found in a human being who truly desires to love others as God loves them. Without His help we can never do it! Ask yourself how well you're doing exhibiting these traits on your own the next time someone cuts you off in traffic, flips you the bird, hurts one of your kids, repeatedly insults you or takes advantage of you; it's hard isn't it?

Let's be honest, it's impossible to do on our own. We can only be 'good' some of the time and that will never measure up to who God calls us to be, which is why He has sent help in the form of His Holy Spirit. Without His Spirit directing your path, giving you perspective and understanding, and giving you a heart for God, you cannot change and can never live a life of peace, joy, and true meaning, and certainly never truly have a selfless view of others. Therefore, you can bless others and invite them to join you on the Kingdom journey so much better when your view of others is properly perceived.

Properly Perceiving What's Next

Are you starting to get it? Your perception of this world can dramatically change when you decide to focus on God, His desire for your life, and His eternal Kingdom. You will continue your life on earth with all the perils and pitfalls it affords, but with a whole new set of eyes. You cannot begin to understand how to do this or manage to change yourself without the help of God. Picture it like this, without Him in your life, it's like you are walking around on earth with a bag over your head. You are managing to survive and make it through day by day but you are missing so very much! He desires to remove that bag from your head and allow you to see things more clearly.

Through His glasses, you will be able to make the right decisions, achieve the goals He has for you while you are here on earth and have a greater love for others. Better yet, you will have the profound joy and excitement of the Kingdom to come and the desire to bring others with you! No longer will this world's trappings keep you from what is truly meaningful and fulfilling. That emptiness and unfulfilled desire inside you will finally be filled and you no longer will see things through the fog of this world, but instead through the light of His eternal Kingdom.

Take this new found truth and make the decision to follow God, ask Him to come into your life and forgive you of your sins and make you clean and new before Him. Tell Him you wish to walk with Him every day from now on. Get yourself a

Bible, join a Bible-believing church, and find others who will walk with you. Ask to be discipled and ask God for the help of His Holy Spirit and to receive the Fruits of the Spirit. Seek Him with all of your heart and see how loving, faithful, forgiving, and kind He is, no matter where you've come from or what you've done! His greatest desire is to walk with you in His eternal Kingdom, start that journey today! Toss off your old glasses and start looking through God's glasses, then and only then will this world truly be properly perceived!

About the Author

Kimberly Underwood is a loving wife to her husband Ben and a blessed mother of three. She is a writer, public speaker, relationship coach and a marriage enhancement facilitator. Kimberly's passion is helping others draw closer to God and experience true change in their lives. She speaks on overcoming a painful past, marriage, divorce, parenting, blended families and adoption. Kimberly resides in Santa Fe, New Mexico.

CPSIA information can be obtained
at www.ICGtesting.com
Printed in the USA
JSHW011322201119
2514JS00001BA/1